High Praise fo

"Environmental writing is often beautiful and moral, but rarely is it as honest as this. Kentucky farmers have Wendell Berry; North Dakota roustabouts have Taylor Brorby."
 —Jeffrey Lockwood, author of *Behind the Carbon Curtain: The Energy Industry, Political Censorship and Free Speech*

"Taylor Brorby has been as tireless as anyone I know in his fight to protect the planet in general, and his beloved high plains of North Dakota in particular. This account of his visits to the Bakken oil fields and to Standing Rock, his acts of resistance and subsequent arrest, is a powerful call to action, a primal scream of anguish and love for the original mother we must now link arms to protect."
 —Pam Houston, author of *Contents May Have Shifted*

"Taylor Brorby's love for his North Dakota homeland resonates in this report from the field of the Standing Rock resistance to the DAPL. As a native son of the land, he speaks with the authority of the heart about protecting the land, the water and the very notion of a sustainable future. He is an important voice in the rising of a new generation dedicated to justice and sustainability."
 —Alison Hawthorne Deming, author of *Stairway to Heaven*

"*Coming Alive* is a moving testimonial to how the industrial invasion of our home landscape can energize a positive ethical and aesthetic response. As he engages in peaceful civil disobedience to protest the environmental and cultural devastation wrought by the Dakota Access Pipeline, Taylor Brorby models the tenacious yet open-hearted resistance that our shared future will require. His thoughtful, personal story of how fracking has devastated his North Dakota homeland is a powerful form of witnessing that we need now more than ever."
 —Michael P. Branch, author of *Raising Wild* and
 Rants from the Hill

"Taylor Brorby's unfiltered meditations about his arrest over the North Dakota Access pipeline lay bare very personal tensions around origins, generations and personal integrity. These play out externally as environmental and social concerns, yet illustrate to the fortunate eavesdropping reader the strength and principle it takes to give in to the demand for an artist to become an activist while learning give up anger—inspired by a "child." Powerful and moving, his thoughts and internal reconciliations are sobering and moving."
 —Ricardo J. Salvador, Director and Senior Scientist,
 Food & Environment Program, Union of Concerned
 Scientists

"Taylor Brorby thought he could escape the Bakken oil boom in his native North Dakota by going away to graduate school in Iowa, but there's no escaping America's hunger for extraction or the pipelines criss-crossing the country. So when the Dakota Access Pipeline began construction across Iowa, a literal link back to the Bakken, Brorby went from writer and self-professed homebody to activist—a role and a label he had long resisted. In *Coming Alive*, he reclaims the word for us all, restoring it to its original meaning: to act, to do—and to do our damnedest to save what's left of our threatened world, one small piece at a time. His vision is broad enough to see the big picture but wise enough to know that lasting battles are only won when we are called to defend the places we live in and love. May Brorby's words inspire each of us 'to do our best work in and for that place.'"

—Ted Genoways, author of *The Chain: Farm, Factory, and the Fate of Our Food*

"Weaving the history of family and prairie, sage grouse and clear water, fury and love, Taylor Brorby's concise manifesto urges us to rededicate ourselves to this insightful truth: when we become thoughtful about emotional lives—our own and others'—we unleash a new and increasingly necessary power."

—Barbara Hurd, author of *Listening to the Savage: River Notes and Half-Heard Melodies*

"Taylor Brorby returns to his native North Dakota to protest the very thing that has in the past sustained him—Big Oil. This first hand account of Standing Rock and fracking takes the reader on a journey across the plains and their environmental devastation. Brorby goes beyond the news clips and sound bites to show us the human story of a young activist caught up in the calamity of a place he calls home. Photos by prize-winning photographer Paul Anderson create the perfect accompaniment to Brorby's stellar prose."

—Mary Swander, author of *Farmscape: The Changing Rural Environment*

Coming Alive

ACTION & CIVIL DISOBEDIENCE

Taylor Brorby
Paul Anderson
Bill McKibben
Kathleen Dean Moore

Ice Cube Press, LLC
North Liberty, Iowa, USA

"Don't ask what the world needs. Ask what makes you come alive, and go do it. Because what the world needs is people who have come alive."
—Howard Thurman

Dedicated to the Protectors,
we are in this together.

Introduction by Bill McKibben

Standing Rock deserves to live beside Lexington and Concord—and Birmingham and Selma—on the honor roll of noble American places. The battle (peaceful on one side) fought there in the fall of 2016 will inform, and push, our history going forward. As this extended essay of Taylor Brorby's makes clear, it has already shaped particular hearts.

That matters came to a head at the confluence of the Missouri and Cannonball rivers didn't particularly surprise me, because I knew many of the people involved. For the last decade, great Native organizers have been leading the fight against the fossil fuel industry on this continent (and on several other continents as well). The reason the tarsands, and with it the Keystone pipeline, became an issue has a great deal to do with organizers like Tom and Dallas Goldtooth or Kandi Mossett or Clayton Thomas-Mueller or Winona LaDuke or Tara Houska, all of whom were in and out of Standing Rock. Underfunded and often ignored by the media, they have patiently built a movement that stretches across national borders and racial and cultural lines.

But Standing Rock also came with remarkable local leaders, women and men who rose to the occasion with grace. (It was LaDonna Allard who welcomed all to her land and began dealing with the impossible logistics; it was local officials like Standing Rock Sioux chairman David Archambault II who proved entirely up to the task of facing off with the federal government.) And it came with followers who poured in from around the country once word began to spread. That influx of bodies is an organizer's dream, and also a nightmare—because who knew who they were, and how they'd react to pressure. Pressure that was applied systematically and brutally by the ever-growing number of police agencies that gathered to protect the pipe and its "right of way." Those authorities understood, instinctively, that if they could just goad the protesters to violence they would win.

But the protesters were having none of it—including the title "protesters." They were, they insisted, "protectors," of the water and the people who depended on it. Their courage in the face of provocation won the day: once the security guards had loosed dogs on them and they'd kept the peace, they were all but invincible.

Their great victory will, of course, be tested in the Trump times, and for the moment the victory may turn to ash. But over the longer run—and time in Indian country has been measured in the longer run—this is a triumph that will stretch over the centuries. It is a signal to the rest of us about what dissent needs to look like now—firm, unyielding, non-violent, rooted in prayer and meditation and music. People of all kinds were drawn inexorably to that campfire, and they will be drawn to the next one.

Bill McKibben is an American environmentalist, author, and journalist who has written extensively on the impact of global warming. He is the Schumann Distinguished Scholar at Middlebury College and leader of the anti-carbon campaign group 350.org. He has authored a dozen books about the environment, including his first, *The End of Nature* (1989), about climate change.

A storm settles in over a Bakken crude shipping facility near Dickinson, North Dakota. The tanker cars are shipped full of Bakken crude to refineries across the United States and Canada.

Coming Alive

Sage swirls around the muddy banks of the Cannon-ball River before it merges with the Missouri River. I've returned home to North Dakota to witness something incredible: the Standing Rock Sioux fight for their sovereignty and stop the Dakota Access Pipeline.

It's a rainy day in August when I pull into the Spirit Camps. My friend Carolyn and I have driven from our home in Ames, Iowa, to bring blankets, jackets, and food to help aid in the battle against the Dakota Access Pipeline, a

1,172 mile pipeline that begins near Stanley, North Dakota, swings west toward Williston, barrels under the Missouri River, crosses South Dakota, and cuts Iowa in half, before connecting to an existing pipeline in Patoka, Illinois.

This damn pipeline has made me into an activist, a label I hate for its politically-heavy association. I moved out of the Bakken oil boom in 2014 to begin writing books and essays about extractive economies, sex trafficking, my home in North Dakota riddled with pump jacks and oil spills. I moved to Ames for graduate school, thinking that, eight hundred miles between the Bakken oil boom and me would be enough space to reflect and rally the troops against the fossil fuel industry. And then, in September, two months after moving to Ames, I first learn about the Dakota Access Pipeline.

In December I attend a public meeting in Ames' City Hall, once an old high school auditorium. Graduate students from Iowa State University, who organized the meeting, direct people, have us fill out name tags, write why we're for clean water and soil rather than oil on poster board. I walk into the auditorium where the stage is filled with various non-profit representatives, an economist from Iowa State

University, and lawyers. I listen to each person give her and his perspective on why we need to stop this pipeline.

I, too, want to stop the pipeline. For the past three years I've traveled around North Dakota, monitored the development and progress of the country's major shale play, the Bakken oil boom. I've read the six major state papers every day for three years. I've kept a file on my computer—"Bakken Project"—with articles about sex trafficking, oil spills, man camps, drug trafficking, infrastructure development. I've lifted weights with roustabouts and wildcatters in Dickinson, and I've seen hats blaze orange with "Big Cock Country" written on them, and t-shirts for sale that say "Going Deep and Pumping Hard" and "Frack That Hole." I've had Americanos at the Boomtown Babes Espresso, a pink drive-thru coffee shop that advertises "The Bakken's Breast Coffee." But no one in the auditorium knows this about me; no one has been to the boom.

I signal to Angie, another graduate student I've met, who's walking around the auditorium with a microphone, monitoring questions and comments. I stand up and face the audience.

"My name is Taylor and I've just moved from the Bakken oil boom." I speak for a few seconds and roll out some figures about pipelines, and I notice Carolyn's eyes are fixed on me. People are paying attention.

When I return home, I'm nervous. I don't want to fight a pipeline. I close my eyes and become dizzy because coal put food on my table in childhood. Brorbys made their fortune by digging luminous lignite coal from the cocoa-colored soil of western North Dakota. When my grandfather was my age, the country didn't know about climate change. James Hansen was still a year away from testifying before Congress about global warming when my mother was pregnant with me—the same age as I am now, twenty-nine. But I now know different. I know the seas are rising, that coal erases the ozone layer, that oil spills contaminate drinking water. I know that my home, western North Dakota, is on fire.

Above my writing desk sits the biblical adage: "To whom much is given, much is expected." Coal paid for vacations to Disney World, saxophone lessons, bicycles, my car, and college. Coal kept my family out of poverty and paid for the boat we'd fish from in the muddy Missouri River. We know coal—and fossil fuels as a whole—do one thing really well: they warm and weird the planet.

Inheritance. My family's love for the outdoors colored by coal, colored by the destruction of the land the adults in my life claimed to love—the Missouri River, the badlands, sage grouse, walleye, paddlefish. I inherited a land I love, and I decide its time for me to fight to protect it.

More than three hundred flags, representing Indigenous Peoples from around the world, line the entrance to the Sacred Stone Spirit Camp at Standing Rock.

As Carolyn and I begin to unload the car, I notice license plates from Washington, Utah, Colorado, Minnesota, New York, Oregon, Wyoming, South Dakota. I hurry back and forth from car to supply tent, loading my arms with the weight of wool. We hear the protest will go through winter. A trained lawyer, Carolyn has come to offer her legal counsel. I've come to stare slack-jawed at the protest in my home state, a state in-bed with the fossil fuel industry.

While Carolyn meets with the Camp's legal team in the supply tent, I go to the open-air medic tent, look at the green-brown hills surrounding the camp. I am the only white man. Dressed in a red Marmot rain jacket and Chacos, I look like the epitome of the granola observer.

"How are things going?" I ask to everyone and no one, immediately wanting to take it back.

"Fine," comes a reply.

"Shitty weather, huh?" *God, Taylor, shut up.*

"Yep."

I unzip my rain jacket and reveal my white-lettered blue t-shirt, which reads, "Stop the Pipeline."

"I've come from Iowa where we're fighting this pipeline. I want to help."

A large man, what the Sioux call a fryboy, looks up from his cell phone, turns to me, and extends his arm. We shake. He goes back to his cell phone.

I stand in the tent, not quite sure what to do. A woman using a garbage bag as a rain jacket comes into the tent. Donna tells me she and her husband have come from the Twin Cities to join the protest and that her daughter is traveling in from Utah tomorrow.

I ask Donna questions—What does it mean for your people to fight this pipeline? Please, tell me your history. What do people need to know about Native struggles? What questions don't white people ask? I hate my ignorance, and ask her questions for hours.

Growing up in coal country, I learned to fear Native Americans. When our little town played basketball against Standing Rock's team our teachers commented that, if we beat them our school would get trashed—garbage cans overturned, windows broken, graffiti lining the hallways. The term "prairie nigger" floated through the hallways.

Earlier in the summer, in July, I travel to Bismarck to visit my sister's family. My nephews—ten, seven, and twin five year-olds—shake the beams of the house and rattle me out of my quiet life. For the past several weeks Logan, the oldest, has been asking his parents about fracking—how it works, what it is, why he hears about it on the news so much. While staying with them, I ask Logan if he'd like to go on a buddy date in the Bakken. We agree to leave the next morning.

Early morning drives in North Dakota ripple with tranquil beauty—a cobalt ocean of sky gives way to a forever-present horizon, occasionally broken by brown buttes or a lonesome grain elevator.

Logan and I decide that his job should be to announce whenever he sees a new flare.

"What's a flare, Uncle Taylor?"

"That, right there," I say as we head north out of Dickinson, one hundred miles into our trip, the southern tip of the oil boom, a blast of orange against a cobalt sky.

We travel to Killdeer Mountain Battlefield, a small historic site west of the town of Killdeer. This place, the battlefield, is where, under the orders of President Lincoln, General Alfred A. Sully attacked Lakota, Nakota, and Dakota peoples. One hundred fifty men, women, and children were killed. Crimson blood flowed across bluebells, milkvetch, sawgrass, the brown palette of the prairie.

Logan has just finished fourth grade. I ask him if he learned about Killdeer Mountain in North Dakota Studies.

"I've never heard of it."

The wide-open prairie of western North Dakota.

Nor had I at his age. I only learned of the battle in my mid-twenties through reading Native American oral accounts. Logan and I kick at the grass, the broken bentonite buttes of the badlands just out of view. I wonder what Logan's thinking, if he thinks the battle is no big deal, another detail kept from the great narrative of American "progress." I want to tell him what school doesn't teach him, how Native Americans are holding up a multi-billion dollar project, how the only way to protect what I value, and want for him—clean water, forests, community—is to stop the one thing corporations value: money. Instead, Logan and I stay silent, soaking in the field before us as pump jacks rock in the distance.

We get back in the car and continue to head north.

"Flare, Uncle Taylor!"

We turn off Highway 22 when I see bulldozers and earth-turned ridges.

"Where are we going?"

"We're going to see what's happening up here. We can't leave the car, okay?"

Logan nods his head.

As we continue down the gravel road, we see construction men. I wave—don't dare smile—and pretend that I know where I'm going. What I don't know is that this road was built only as an access to build this pipeline.

"There it is, Logan."

"What?"

"That's the pipeline that will go all the way to Illinois. It can carry twenty-five million gallons of oil a day."

Just ahead is green pipe, set up in piles, laid out over the broken prairie, chocolate earth turned over to make a bed for the pipeline. I pull off the road onto an approach and snap a few pictures. I see the construction workers stop what they're doing and look at us. I wave. *Why the fuck did I wave?*

"Another flare, Uncle Taylor," and I feel Logan pull on my shirt.

"Yep, buddy. We gotta go." I drop my camera and return onto the road. We get back onto Highway 22 and continue north. No construction workers follow us.

"More flares."

"How many is that?"

"Thirty-three."

I reach for my coffee. We drive past bentonite badlands—brown, orange, streaked pink from scoria and black from coal—and cross onto the Fort Berthold Reservation.

"There are still Native Americans, Uncle Taylor? I thought they were all dead."

I don't know what to say. First, I think that maybe my nephew is one of the few blessed people who doesn't see race; I mean, my god, his best friend is half-Native American. But then I think more and get angry—maybe his teachers have only taught him the history of Custer, whom I sang songs about in my own childhood, or Lewis and Clark, who, sixty miles from here, survived due only to the generosity of the Mandan people.

I breathe in. "This is where some Native Americans in North Dakota call home. Native Americans are still alive." I roll Logan's comment around in my head, click my fingers on the steering wheel. It's not him I'm mad at, it's the People in Charge that shape mythic narratives.

"More flares, Uncle Taylor," and an ocean of fire spreads before us. We drive along Lake Sakakawea, singing along to Bruno Mars, Lady Gaga, and Sia. We stop for lunch in Williston, known as Boomtown, USA, at a Subway. Pickup trucks line the parking lot, some with metal testicles hanging from the hitches. I put my arm around Logan as we walk into Subway.

"Tell the lady what you want, Logan."

"A foot-long Philly cheesesteak."

"Are you sure you can eat a foot-long, buddy?"

Silence.

"I'll have one, too."

I struggle to eat mine as Logan licks his fingers.

"I'm a growing boy, Uncle Taylor."

"Yes, I know. I only grow horizontally now. Go wash your fingers."

As I look around I think of what the oil boom has done to Williston. A quiet town a decade ago, Williston has doubled in size. New gas stations, hotels, grocery stores line the street. But with the falling price of oil, times turn difficult in a town where people used to make seventeen dollars an hour at Wal-Mart.

I check the time, look around the restaurant—mom and dad, two daughters. Two oil workers silently eat together. I wonder about the upcoming election, about what will happen if Trump takes office, or what will happen if he doesn't. What does the world need right now? I swirl my finger on the plastic table. I turn over and over my frustration in my head. Why is it so difficult to be good, to not harm the things I love?

I look at the oil workers, crafting a narrative of how they need this work, how they need to, somehow, provide for themselves and their families; how they're from out of state and have no choice. I know this boom is not their fault.

And yet I want to sink the oil industry, to tell these workers that their jobs can—and will—go away, that ruining the planet isn't an honest way to make a living. I want to sit with them and tell them that their health is at stake, that we need better leaders to help us provide stable, sunshine powered jobs so their children still have a world to fall in love with, rather than one ruined by free market economics. But how do to you tell the victims of corporate greed not to feed their families, not to save for retirement, how to leave this job and, somehow, find other work?

Logan returns, whipping his hands on his jersey shorts.

"My turn. Can you watch my stuff, buddy?"

While urinating, I panic. Shit. I've left him alone. I try to hurry. Figures of missing children race through my head. My sister! My sister! Oh god! I nip myself. I wash my hands, trembling. I've left my nephew alone in the oil boom!

I rip open the door and it slams against the wall. Everyone looks at me. Logan is refilling our sodas.

"Why are you sweating, Uncle Taylor?"

"Wasn't it hot in there to you?"

"No."

We leave Subway and swing south out of Williston and cross the Missouri River. More flares. Eventually we end up west of Killdeer Mountain.

"We've made one big circle today."

"Yes we have, buddy. How about a dip into the badlands?"

"Yes!"

We pull off Highway 85 and enter the Little Missouri National Grasslands. North Dakota contains nearly one-third of the nation's 3.8 million acres of the National Grasslands, an ocean of grass under a sea of sky.

"Another flare, Uncle Taylor!"

Carved by Master Carver Jewell James, a totem pole passes
bentonite mounds after leaving the Sacred Stone Spirit Camp
near Standing Rock. An act of support, the totem pole was
transported as part of the effort to minimize damage from the
fossil fuel industry to the land.

The road swings down between two bluffs. I slow the car and we hit strawberry-colored scoria roadway. I slow some more. We curve around a bend and there it is—a gray, red, black, beige bentonite bluff. Sixty-five million years of earth's work, leveled like a dining table, a pump jack bobbing up and down up and down, like a chicken pecking at scratch.

The car idles. Eventually I kill the motor. A moment passes, an eternity.

"Our bluffs are never coming back, Uncle Taylor."

Our second and last day at the Camp Carolyn and I again split up. I meet Betsy, a retired Boeing worker and native North Dakotan, from Washington State. We walk to the Cannonball River for a boat launch. Boaters will paddle into the Missouri River, praying along the way. Song, chant, prayer flow over the water. I join others atop the bridge to watch the ceremony. Flags snap in the breeze, oars smack glistening water.

I walk back to Camp with Betsy.

"You're looking red," she says, and offers me some sunscreen.

"White men burn easy out here" a man yells at me. We chuckle. I see Donna and wave.

"Come meet my family!" she waves me over. I meet Donna's husband, their daughter Iktomi Was'te Wigan (Good Spider Woman), who fights fracking in Utah. We sit and share our struggles—mine in this place, North Dakota, fighting the industry that put bread and milk on my table in childhood, and she, in Utah, against an industry attempting to erase her and her culture. A woman passes, carrying a bucket of smoking sage, and we wash ourselves in the perfume of the prairie.

Iktomi Was'te Wigan gets up to stretch and I leave to use the porta potty. Afterward, I stop by a car from Oregon, slathered in bumper stickers: "Stop Public Lands Ranching," "Visualize Industrial Collapse," "Subvert the Dominant Paradigm," "You Cannot Simultaneously Prevent and Prepare for War," "I ♥ Mountains," "A world of wanted children would make a world of difference."

I return to the tent and sit in my camp chair. A small girl with cropped brown hair, perhaps five or six, comes skipping through. Her shirt, riven with gems, has the word "love" splayed over her chest. She skips as if to pass by me— stops, pivots, stares directly into my eyes. Her chocolate brown eyes narrow.

"It's time to let go of anger." She skips on. I wipe my face.

A few minutes later Iktomi Was'te Wigan returns. I tell her what just happened.

"Oh my god, Taylor, that little girl came up to me on walk, pointed to our tent and said, 'Someone in that tent is angry' and skipped away."

"We're all angry," I say.

"Yes, but you white people look really angry." We laugh.

Carolyn and I meet at the car to leave Camp, exhausted at the work done and the work to come. We head north on Highway 1806. We stop at the Dakota Access construction site. The fence, lined with tribal flags, bursts with color in the late afternoon sun. On the approach to the construction site are two make-shift tipi frames, on one side sits a sign that reads "Mni-Wiconi Water IS Life" in blue and white paint, on the other side another sign, "No more stolen sisters" in white and black paint. An upside down United States flag—the universal signal for distress—flows in the wind. At the entrance to the construction site another sign in simple red lettering: No Access for Dakota Access.

We hop out of the car, both of us in our blue "Stop the Pipeline" t-shirts. I snap a picture of Carolyn. She does the same for me.

"Ready, Taylor? Three-two-one."

I flip off the construction site.

JoDe Goudy, Chairman of the Yakama Nation leads the Washington State Chiefs and Lummi totem pole across the Cannonball River and into the Sacred Stone Spirit Camp, Standing Rock, North Dakota.

On August 31 in Pilot Mound, Iowa, forty-five minutes northwest of my home in Ames, the Bakken Pipeline Resistance Coalition, a grassroots group fighting the Dakota Access Pipeline, holds a meeting for a nonviolent, direct action training against the pipeline. I ride along with Carolyn.

In Pilot Mound we listen to a lawyer about potential outcomes if arrested. We hear veteran protestors share stories of being arrested. We listen to Frank, the leader of the training, guide us through what we are to do.

"We're here to demonstrate. If you're here to cause trouble, we don't want you. Now is your time to leave."

We continue on for an hour. Ed, the leader of Bold Iowa, one of the members of the Coalition, asks those who came to risk arrest today to please stand. In emails, I'm told that Bold Iowa expects a low turn-out at the event—maybe thirty of us, and that ten would probably risk arrest. Today there are one hundred people in the community center at Pilot Mound.

Thirty-six of us stand. A pen falls to the floor. I wipe my eyes.

"Stay standing," says Ed. "If you aren't able to risk arrest today and are willing to risk it at a later time, would you please stand?"

Another twenty-five rise. The room erupts in cheers.

Frank leads us through a series of role-playing exercises. I partner-up with a man named Chris, a bicycle mechanic from Cedar Rapids.

"One of you will be a protestor, the other will be law enforcement."

"You're older," I whisper to Chris, "I think you should play law enforcement first." I sit on the floor, imagining I'm blocking construction.

"Now listen here, young man, it doesn't matter what you do. We're building this pipeline no matter what."

I stay silent, choosing not to engage with Chris, the pretend-police-officer.

"Time to go. You don't want this on your record."

I flinch. He's right. I don't want this on my record. I don't want to have to explain to potential employers why I was arrested for wanting clean water. Standing Rock flashes through my mind. And then, one by one, my four nephews, right in the path of this pipeline. I stay silent.

Chris has run out of harassment phrases and shrugs. We giggle. He sits down, his turn to protest.

"Now listen here, old man." Chris raises his eyebrows. "Oh, did that get you upset? Well, you're not going to be happy spending a night in the slammer! Can you even afford bail, you little environmentalist hippie?" My chest heaves; I think of what I would never want to hear in this moment. "You don't matter. This pipeline's a done deal. You can't stop it. No one will remember what happened here. Get up."

Chris sits still, mumbles, "I ain't moving."

"What's that? You think this matters? You think you matter?" I turn red and continue the assault.

"All right, that's enough," Frank hollers. I help Chris up and we pat each other on the back. We continue training for another hour before breaking for a potluck lunch.

I can't eat and, instead, wander around. I decide to go outside to the playground and swing on the swing set. A father and his infant son swing too. A little girl comes up to me.

"Hey, are you getting arrested today?"

"I hope not. But I will if I have to."

"Thanks!" She waves and runs away.

Carolyn waves me in. It's go time.

"All ready?" Frank yells. "Let's do this."

A long caravan leaves Pilot Mound, heading south to Boone, the exact middle point of the Iowa section of the pipeline.

"Look at that," Carolyn says.

I look in the rearview mirror. Cars, trucks, vans as far as I can see. People waving to each other, honking. We dip into the Des Moines River Valley and see where the pipe will cross under the river. Mocha-colored earth is over-turned, a section of trees, clear-cut.

"That poor farmer has to look at this every day," says Carolyn.

We continue toward Boone. During the meeting the leaders of Coalition decided we'd block the assembly site for the pipeline near Boone, where hundreds of farmers are gathered at the fairgrounds for the Farm Progress Show.

As we turn into the fairgrounds we see state troopers. We host a rally, listen to landowners bemoan the destruction of their land, and we begin walking in the ditch toward the construction site. I spread my fingers and feel the tall prairie grass as the sun warms my back.

Those willing to risk arrest break off into groups of nine at the four entrances to the construction site, enough people to prevent machinery from exiting and entering the assembly site.

"Good luck, Group Four!" a supporter shouts.

Groups Three and Two take their places at each entrance. I am in Group One, joining my new friend Julia and old friend Jan, a retired professor.

As we approach our entrance, my heart slams over and over. We leave the ditch and the white gravel crunches below our feet. I am at the far end of our group. We join hands, nine of us spreading ourselves across the entrance, a human wall blocking metal machines.

Click, click, click. A flash here, a news anchor there. We're documented. Our story ripples across the web.

I turn to Julia. "How do you feel?"

"I'm nervous."

I squeeze her hand tight. "Hey, nothing's going to happen. I'm right here. I'm not going anywhere."

What I thought would be a quick procedure drags on. Naively, I thought we'd trespass, get cuffed, and then be hauled off to jail. The troopers don't move. *Damn, I knew I should've gone to the bathroom.*

A woman with sunglasses and white hair waves to us.

"Who's that?"

"That's my mom," says Julia.

I wonder what my own mother would say if she could see me now, risking arrest, trying to stop a pipeline. We haven't spoken in months. My activism a difficult thing for her to swallow.

"What do you think she's thinking?"

"She probably thinks I'm crazy."

"I bet she's really proud," and I squeeze Julia's hand. A tear sizzles on the gravel.

I see Frank cup his mouth. "All right, this is it!"

The lead State Trooper tells us that anyone who stays will be arrested. I grip Julia's hand. Here we go. No one steps out from our line. I look straight ahead and see Carolyn taking notes.

I feel a tug on my arm, and my hand falls away from Julia. The slamming in my chest quickens. In and out, in and out. I focus on breathing. And then I see her—no one else does, but I do—the child from Standing Rock. I know then, *It's time to let go of anger*. I smile.

"3:30PM and you're the first one to be arrested, Taylor," shouts Carolyn.

"Are the cuffs too tight, sir?" asks the trooper.

"No." I smirk, thinking, *I've always wanted a big, strong man to put my arms behind my back*.

I'm turned around and led back behind the earthen berm, away from my friends, out of the media's sight. More officers are waiting.

"Hello, sir." The officer asks me my name. "Mr. Brorby, we're going to take your possessions and pat you down."

Away goes my belt, my blue Minnesota Twins hat, my pocket change.

"What's this?"

"That's my insulin pump. You can take it, but then we'll really have some trouble."

I can tell now is not the time for humor. Every part of me—every part of me—is pat down before I am loaded into the back of the van. Stepping up and navigating to the back of the van proves difficult. I wobble, unable to use my hands for balance. I'm hunched over, suddenly feel old as I slowly turn, then sit, leaning forward so as to not press my arms. The officer turns on the air.

One by one I see other protestors led to my van. Mariam, part of the group 100 Grannies for a Livable Future, squeezes next to me in the back of the van. She's been given the fashionable zip ties to bind her hands.

"Those look more comfortable," I say.

She rolls her eyes.

Jan joins us in the van, sitting in front of me in a bucket seat. Kathy, from Iowa City, joins Mariam and me in the back. The last one to join us is a middle-aged man, Nick. Nick, we soon find out, is prone to motion sickness.

We make it to the Boone County Jail. One by one we exit the van, a little uncertain of how to walk. When our cuffs are removed, Jan and I moan and swing our arms.

"Damn, I should really do more shoulder exercises if I'm going to be arrested" I say.

Jan and I are moved into a temporary cell, now wearing flip-flops—mine pink, his yellow—since our footwear has been taken away.

"You can use that drain if you need to go to the bathroom," says the officer.

"I'm afraid I need to use it, Jan."

Jan stays in front of me. I've never pissed before another human before while trying to maintain eye contact, hit the drain, and have polite conversation. I think, there must be a gold medal for this.

"Have you ever been arrested before, Jan?" I want him to talk so I can finish my business.

"The last time was in the Sixties when we tried to levitate the Pentagon."

We spend the evening in the Boone County Jail with thirteen other men who are arrested. The officer, whom we nickname Barney Fife, tells us this is the largest single arrest in his forty years at the jail. We eat bologna sandwiches on white bread, a slice of Kraft American cheese for plastic flavor. Cheetos, a cookie, an apple, a pint of two percent milk. We ebb and flow between conversation and silence, surrounded by white cinderblock walls, a perpetually open bathroom door, showers without metal rings—to help prevent injury—steel chairs attached to steel tables. It takes awhile and then I realize everything here has been engineered, been thought through for potential injury or weaponry. I am in one of the most thought-out environments. The television whizzes in the background.

"Tonight, at six, thirty people arrested in Boone County, attempting to block the Dakota Access Pipeline," booms the anchor's voice.

Someone turns up the volume.

The news story centers around Julia, the young female farmer. Later, while being fingerprinted, I tell Julia and the other women about the news. The men are held in the back of the jail in one of the two pods designated for longer-term inmates. We've displaced an entire group of inmates. The women are held up front, in cells similar to the one's where Jan and I were first held.

"Of course," says Julia. "Focus on the young woman." She rolls her eyes.

When I return to the pod, I sit off to the side by myself, realizing I haven't checked my blood sugar in over six hours. I don't have access to my medical supplies. How long will they hold me?

Later at night we hear footsteps coming down the hallway of the jail. Barney Fife opens the door.

"Mr. Brorby," he waves for me to follow him.

I'm the first one released from the day of protesting. Carolyn has posted my bail and, seven hours after I'm arrested, I'm freed—but not before being told the jail has misplaced my possessions.

I walk out into the warm night air, shoeless, joking that I feel like Jesus. Friends snap pictures on their phones. Carolyn and I begin the drive home under the inky Iowa sky, stars glistening every now and then.

Once home, I go to my room, set my phone on the pile of books next to my bed. I turn it off and cry. My shoulders heave as tears hit my bed sheet, then books. Some splatter my toes. Since entering the fray over fracking, I've only felt anger—I've raged against hijacked politics, traveled the country to lecture against destructive industry, and have been consumed by writing about fracking.

I close my eyes and see the switchgrass swaying in the wind at Standing Rock. The muddy Cannonball River gurgles its way to the Missouri River. I hear singing, I hear prayer, I hear chanting. The world made new and the task before us: the resistance against the ruin of every living thing, the building of community beyond boardrooms and backroom deals, the ability to stand as witnesses, protectors, and activists to build an imaginative future forward, one where clean water flows. And then I see her again, the child. I cry some more, realizing I've now come back to being fully human as my anger slips away.

I never intended to be an activist—the label usually put upon me by others. If you get arrested, surely you must be an activist. What I really want to be is a homebody—to read, write, and struggle to make art. But my home in North Dakota is on fire—flares fume across the mixed grass prairie, bentonite bluffs are leveled and pumped to bleed oil, the Missouri River, the artery of the continent, now contains radioactive material. The pallid sturgeon is predicted to go extinct in my lifetime, the sage grouse is consistently threatened. My home in Iowa, devastated by industrial agriculture, now faces one of the nation's largest pipelines going under its eight major waterways. Water, in Iowa, already toxic due to nitrate runoff, stands to be ruined by a rupture in the Dakota Access Pipeline. I close my eyes when I think of these things and become dizzy.

I keep coming back to that word—activist—wanting to pick at it like a bur in the saddle. The root meaning of activist means "to drive, to do." What I'm driving at is a world of diversity, a world where my being gay doesn't preclude me from living in certain parts of the country, where being black doesn't mean living in fear of being stopped by police for a ticket, where strong women are celebrated, where Native sovereignty is a right, just like clean drinking water. I try to live out my own ideals, why doesn't this country live up to its ideals?

I'm driving at a world of diversity because we know nature flourishes with many species—just like humans do—rather than a few. The prairie I love is a web of intimate and interconnected roots that secure topsoil, which provides clean water, which creates healthy fisheries, which feed mammals and birds. We cannot separate our thinking from the tapestry of life—once one thread is loosed, the whole unravels.

But activism also means "to do." I do not expect each of us to take up the banner of fighting fracking like I have. In

A pump jack extracts oil near a Bakken oil loading facility in North Dakota.

fact, I do not expect us to model our lives after mine; after all, I must admit I would probably not be fierce in the fight against fracking if it weren't destroying the very place I love. But each of us comes from a place, a place that might be very different from my place, one with its own struggles and unique circumstances.

Here's what I need: I need each of us to do our best work in and for our places. You must trust I am trying my damnedest in the fight against fracking, and I will trust you are doing your best work on your own front. After all, a tapestry is not one thread but many; if we all weave together in our own way, the whole becomes tighter, the tapestry stronger.

I do not know how to help salmon fisheries in the Northwest, but my friend David does. I do not know the injustice of the for-profit prison system, but my friend Shane does. My friend Jenny writes poems to wake us up about the complexities of queerness in the animal kingdom. Darren produces photography that complicates our understanding of masculinity. Lauret weaves narratives of nature and multi-ethnic identity to help seek justice. I suck at any of these things, but I need these friends to do their good work in their own ways, which gives me permission to act, which is really all an activist is—a person who acts.

But I worry activist has taken on a negative meaning. Is it bad of me to protect the waterways I depend upon in Iowa for clean drinking water by attempting to stop a pipeline? Is it bad that I want the sage grouse and pallid sturgeon to continue to live in North Dakota? Is it bad that I write letters-to-the-editor about the risks of breathing in air tainted by flaring? Is it bad to believe that the Missouri River should be free of radioactive material? Why is wanting a diverse and clean planet so damn controversial?

If the American Spirit is to thrive in the 21st century, it must come from our relationship to place and to each other. At a time when it feels so easy to close ourselves off from the rest of the world and the planet we so desperately depend upon, radical reaching out towards community, compassion, and creativity is what is needed. The world does not need any more coal plants, natural gas pipelines, or oil booms. The world needs people with the imagination to help us see clearly the world we are a part of, and how we might live better with and in our places.

Through the development of extractive economies, humanity's ability to live on the planet totters. Will we fall off of the ledge or work with the new climate unfolding on Earth? Places, and our relationship to them, do not exist outside of ourselves—they dwell deep within us. Each of us lives in a place and a place in us, and it is through knowing our places that we come to know ourselves and each other—our hopes and dreams, our fears, and our ability to dig into the work that lies ahead resides in place. It's in this type of work where we build relationships with people whose narratives are different from ours. It's in this place of relationship where our world grows and our work builds upon each other.

The work on behalf of the planet is even more daunting now. People of color and those living in coastal areas are disproportionally affected by climate change. To work on behalf of each other and the planet is to work for justice; to rely on Wall Street and corporations is poison. The work that needs doing will come from the ground up, and it will be a movement lead by people—not politicians—doing the work that needs to be done in place and with each other. Perhaps the reason the public has not taken the issue of climate change seriously is because scientists, academics, and experts go about their business and work as usual. If these vicars of knowledge and objectivity took themselves seriously, they'd be in the streets, at public meetings, disrupting the status quo, overwhelming the world with the knowledge we need to make meaningful change and to elect leaders that inspire imaginative thinking rather than fear.

And this work will be hard and difficult, this work will look like Standing Rock—people willing to dig in for the long haul, putting bodies on the line, fighting for what's right during all manner of weather. This work will not take place in cushy boardrooms or over retreat weekends, it will take place when all voices are heard.

This intricate move of coming alive is now before us. To come alive means to pay attention, to notice, to understand a thing well and then to act. Inaction breeds destruction. Coming alive is a way of noticing, a way of listening, it is to understand one's responsibility to others, even nonhuman others, and then to act in a sacred way of radiating outward, of growing magnanimous.

Recently, where selfishness and fear have thrived in this country, a type of radical awakening to prevent the destruction of the planet and our own humanity is emerging. We are now in the arena, and the fight before us must be led with compassion and song, prayer and joy, and a fire for justice that spreads far and wide.

Afterword: All Hands
by Kathleen Dean Moore

When a fearsome storm is bearing down on a great ship—the first winds shuddering in the sails, the first waves burying the bowsprit, sullen clouds obscuring the horizon—the captain shouts the order. "All hands on deck." Every sailor knows what that means. Each person on board, no matter their rank or watch, has an absolute duty to rush, from their gambling tables or bunks, to their stations to do whatever has to be done to save the ship. If the captain is incompetent or irresponsible, the "All Hands!" cry is a panicked shout from every quarter into the face of the storm.

What if sailors don't respond?—"Give me a minute, I've got some lucky dice for once." Or, "wake me if it gets really bad." Under the old laws of the sea, that would be a flogging offense, or worse. But the failure to respond would be a moral transgression as well—in two ways. First, the crew members who do not respond become free riders, taking unearned advantage of the actions of those who do answer the call. But worse, those who do not respond say, by their

lassitude, that they don't believe the crisis is real and imme-
diate. If their inaction persuades too many others, who will
right the ship?

The analogy is a harsh one. The climate disruptions
that are bearing down on the planet—intense heat, floods
and droughts, failed crops, waves of desperate refugees,
extinctions, and acidified seas—are a planetary emergency.
Unaddressed, they could take down the ship.

"Unless immediate action is taken," three hundred
scientists recently wrote, "by the time today's children are
middle-aged, the life support systems of the planet will be
irretrievably damaged." This is a call for all hands on deck.
Given the silence or perfidy of government "leaders," the
call is coming from all quarters—scientists, religious lead-
ers, human rights activists, national security advisors, econ-
omists, parents, and local government officials, including
indigenous people worldwide. Turning back this crisis, if it
is still possible, will take the greatest and most determined
public collective action the planet has ever seen.

The danger is that inattentive citizens might not step
up to help. And that is a moral failure; let us say it straight.
Those who stand aside are taking advantage of the actions,
often sacrifices, of those who step up to demand or offer
solutions. If the children of the inattentive have fresh
drinking water, if their grandchildren have enough to eat,
if their coastline property fends off the rising seas, it will

be because of the courage of others, not their own. But the inattentive are not just doing nothing. It's worse than that. Their silence reinforces the message that this climate disruption is no big deal—exactly the message the fossil fuel industries and their government minions want to convey. In that way, those who fail to respond to the emergency call, those just strolling along—*la de da, whatever*—become part of the storm itself.

Here's the point: Democracies are governments by and for the vociferous—the shouters and tweeters, yes, but also the people who pack the meeting halls and pick up the phones. When people show up for the cause, they win, as we have seen again and again, for better or for worse. When they don't, they lose. In the United States, a significant majority, sixty-one percent of voters, think that climate disruption is an "extremely," "very," or "moderately" important issue. But of those, more than half "rarely" or "never" even talk about it.

This book is a call to all hands to rush on deck, to "come alive" to help save what they care about the most, by doing what they do best. Is it writing? Is it speaking? Is it singing? Is it organizing? Is it walking in a parade? Is it even blocking a bulldozer? There might have been a time when our work for the world was quiet work in our private lives, focused on exemplary living and careful consumption. That time has passed. Now our work is in the streets, in the state houses, on the riverbanks, in the college quad, in the grocery line, speaking out. Speaking out against the corporate plunder of the planet. Raising our voices to defend the endangered beings who have no voice to defend themselves—future generations, plants and animals, the desperate poor, the children.

Kathleen Dean Moore is a philosopher, writer, and environmental activist from Oregon State University. Her early creative nonfiction writing focused on the cultural and spiritual values of the natural world, especially shorelines and islands. Her more recent work is about the moral issues of climate change.

A thunderstorm developing over the plains of eastern Montana.

Paul Anderson is an environmental, documentary, land-scape and editorial photographer from Northwest Washington. His photos have been published around the world. Clients include *National Geographic*, the *New York Times*, *USA Today*, *The Nation*, *The Economist*, *Sierra Club*, *NRDC*, *Waterkeeper Magazine*, *Huffington Post*, *Yes Magazine*, *Sightline*, *Sierra Magazine*, *Bloomberg Business Week*, *Greenpeace*, *National Wildlife Federation*, *Climate Solutions*, *Grist* and hundreds of other newspapers, magazines, businesses, government organizations, and nonprofits. He has been an avid photographer, climber, hiker, rugby player, sailor, kayaker for much of his life. Born and raised in Davenport, Iowa, he now lives in Bellingham, WA, close to the Salish Sea, North Cascades, and the San Juan Archipelago. Fmi: www.paulkanderson.com

Taylor Brorby is an award-winning essayist, and a poet. A fellow at the Black Earth Institute, Taylor's work has appeared in numerous journals and magazines, including *Orion, High Country News, The Huffington Post,* and *Terrain.org,* and has received numerous recognitions through grants and artist residencies.

Taylor travels around the country regularly to speak about hydraulic fracking, is a co-editor of the country's first anthology of creative writing about fracking, *Fracture: Essays, Poems, and Stories on Fracking in America,* and is Reviews Editor at *Orion Magazine.* His poetry collection, *Crude,* is coming out in the spring of 2017.

The Ice Cube Press began publishing in 1993 to focus on how to live with the natural world. We've since become devoted to using the literary arts to better understand how people can best live together in the communities they share, inhabit, and experience here in the Heartland of the USA. We have been recognized by a number of well-known writers including: Gary Snyder, Gene Logsdon, Wes Jackson, Patricia Hampl, Greg Brown, Jim Harrison, Annie Dillard, Ken Burns, Roz Chast, Jane Hamilton, Daniel Menaker, Kathleen Norris, Janisse Ray, Robert Hass, Alison Deming, Frank Deford, Paul Hawken, Harriet Lerner, Richard Rhodes, Michael Pollan, David Abram, David Orr, Boria Sax, and Barry Lopez. We've published a number of well-known authors including: Governor Robert Ray, Congressman James Leach, Mary Swander, Jim Heynen, Mary Pipher, Bill Holm, Connie Mutel, John T. Price, Carol Bly, Marvin Bell, Debra Marquart, Ted Kooser, Stephanie Mills, Bill McKibben, Craig Lesley, Elizabeth McCracken, Dean Bakopoulos, Dan Gable, Rick Bass, Pam Houston, and Paul Gruchow. Check out Ice Cube Press books on our web site, join our facebook group, follow us on twitter, visit booksellers, museum shops, or any place you can find good books and discover why we continue striving to, "hear the other side."

Ice Cube Press, LLC (Est. 1993)
North Liberty, Iowa 52317-9302
steve@icecubepress.com
twitter: @icecubepress
www.facebook.com/IceCubePress
www.IceCubePress.com

to Laura Lee & Fenna Marie
holding on to
wishes hopes & dreams
no matter what!